# UNICORN

## Color by Sight Word

**Sparkling Minds**

# SIGHT WORDS
## Pre-K

| | | | |
|---|---|---|---|
| a | funny | look | see |
| and | go | make | the |
| away | help | me | three |
| big | here | my | to |
| blue | I | not | two |
| can | in | one | up |
| come | is | play | we |
| down | it | red | where |
| find | jump | run | yellow |
| for | little | said | you |

# Kindergarten

| | | | |
|---|---|---|---|
| all | four | out | this |
| am | get | please | too |
| are | good | pretty | under |
| at | have | ran | want |
| ate | he | ride | was |
| be | into | saw | well |
| black | like | say | went |
| brown | must | she | what |
| but | new | so | white |
| came | no | soon | who |
| did | now | that | will |
| do | on | there | with |
| eat | our | they | yes |

# First Grade

| | | | |
|---|---|---|---|
| after | give | let | some |
| again | going | live | stop |
| an | had | may | take |
| any | has | of | thank |
| as | her | old | them |
| ask | him | once | then |
| by | his | open | think |
| could | how | over | walk |
| every | just | put | were |
| fly | know | round | when |
| from | | | |

# Second Grade

| | | | |
|---|---|---|---|
| always | don't | or | upon |
| around | fast | pull | us |
| because | first | read | use |
| been | five | right | very |
| before | found | sing | wash |
| best | gave | sit | which |
| both | goes | sleep | why |
| buy | green | tell | wish |
| call | its | their | work |
| cold | made | these | would |
| does | many | those | write |
| | off | | your |

the - light blue    to - dark pink    and - light purple    a - dark blue

one - red    my - light pink    me - yellow    big - dark purple

said - light blue     for - light pink     up - orange     look - red

jump - light purple     away - yellow     here - dark pink     help - dark purple

see - orange      not - dark blue      is - light blue      go - red

funny - light purple      three - light pink      yellow - dark purple      make - yellow

two - light blue    little - orange    down - light purple    run - light pink

we - dark pink    play - brown    find - yellow    can - dark blue

I - dark purple    blue - yellow    red - light blue    come - orange

you - dark pink    it - red    in - light purple    where - light green

see - red

funny - dark pink

he - light purple

she - dark purple

three - dark blue

not - light pink

that - orange

now - yellow

there - orange     out - yellow     be - light purple     have - dark blue

saw - red     well - light green     ran - light blue     brown - dark pink

but - orange     at - yellow     four - dark pink     pretty - light purple

want - light blue     too - dark purple     all - red     with - light pink

no - light pink    came - light blue    on - dark purple    was - light purple

they - dark blue    ride - orange    into - yellow    good - dark pink

am - dark green      eat - dark pink      did - light purple      must - light blue

who - yellow      new - dark purple      what - orange      do - light green

are - light purple    this - orange    like - yellow    soon - light green

get - dark purple    yes - dark blue    so - light blue    black - light pink

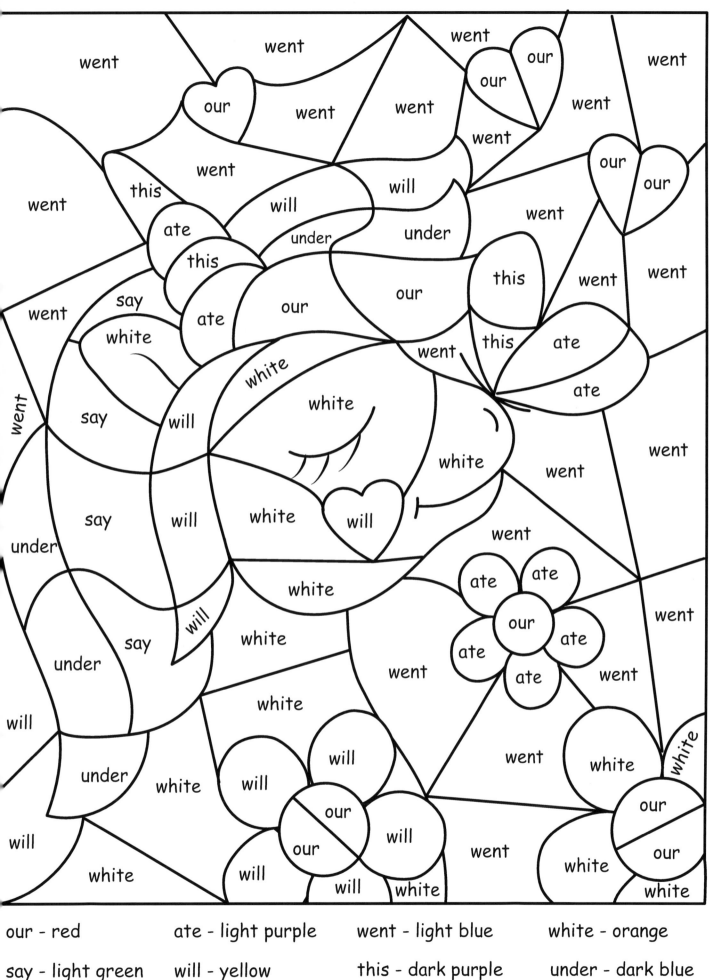

our - red       ate - light purple       went - light blue       white - orange

say - light green     will - yellow       this - dark purple      under - dark blue

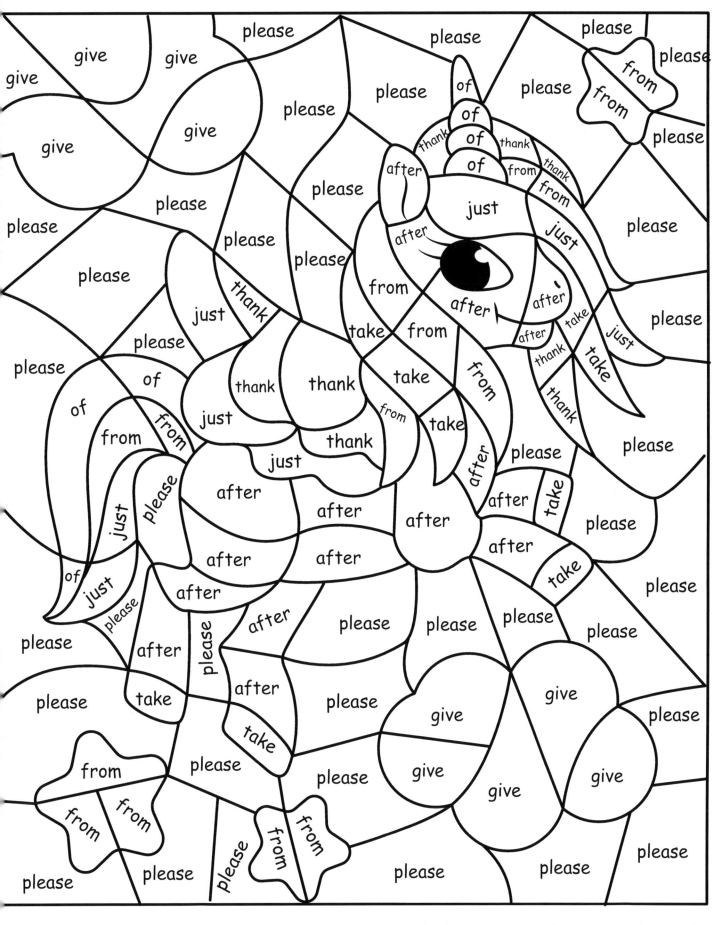

from - yellow      thank - dark blue      just - dark pink      please - dark purple

take - orange      of - light purple      give - light blue      after - light pink

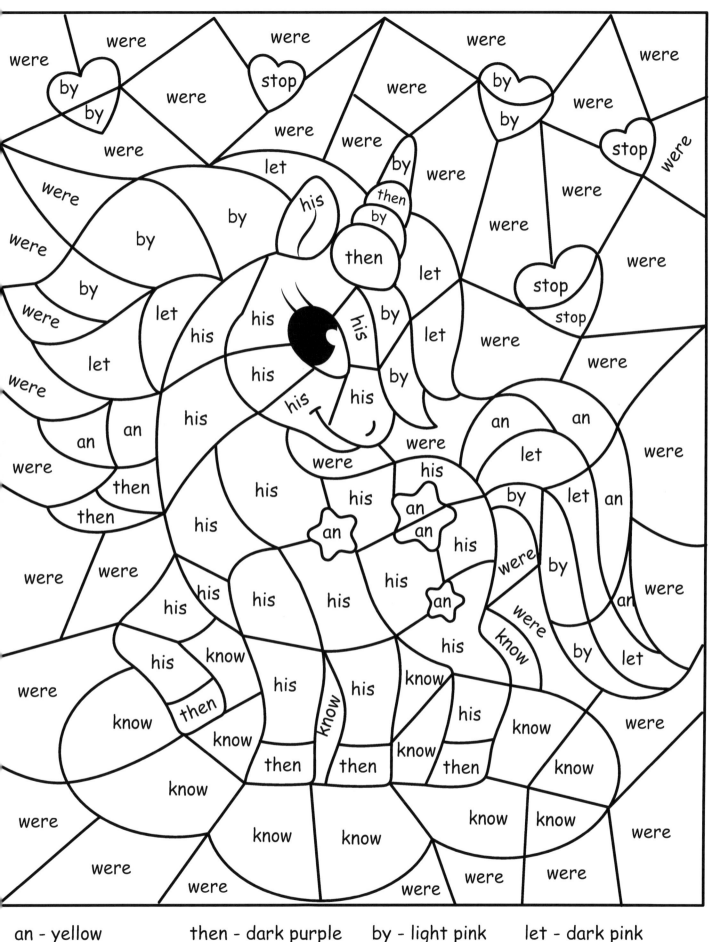

an - yellow          then - dark purple          by - light pink          let - dark pink

his - light purple          were - dark green          stop - red          know - light green

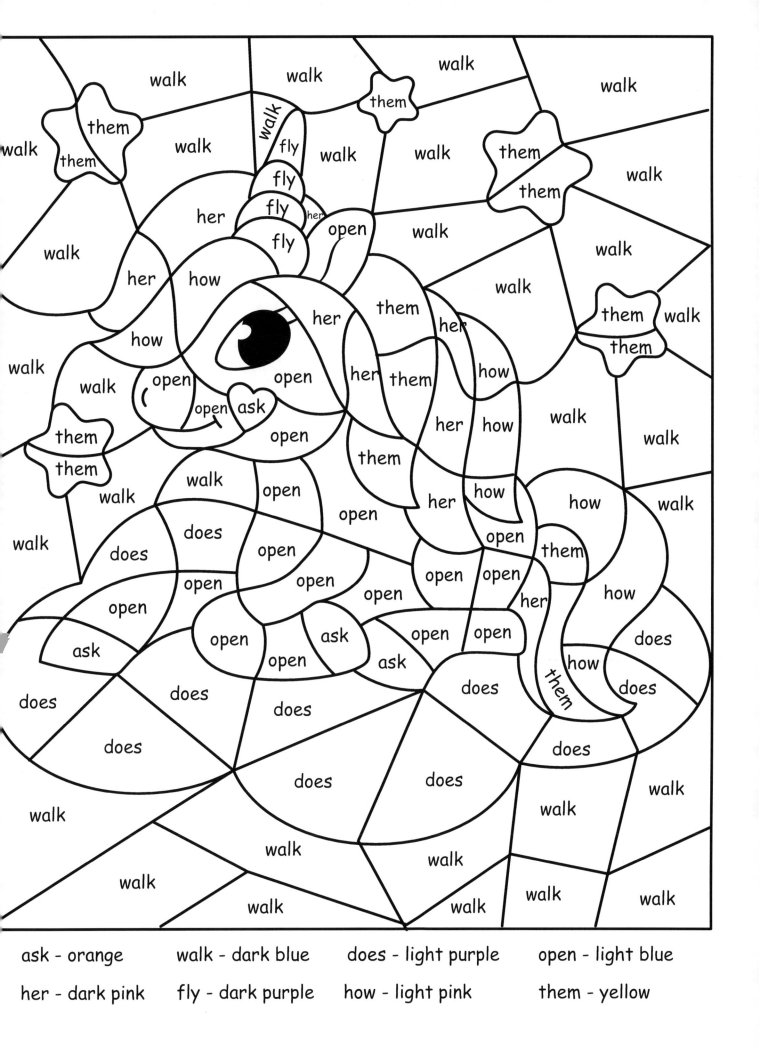

ask - orange     walk - dark blue     does - light purple     open - light blue

her - dark pink     fly - dark purple     how - light pink     them - yellow

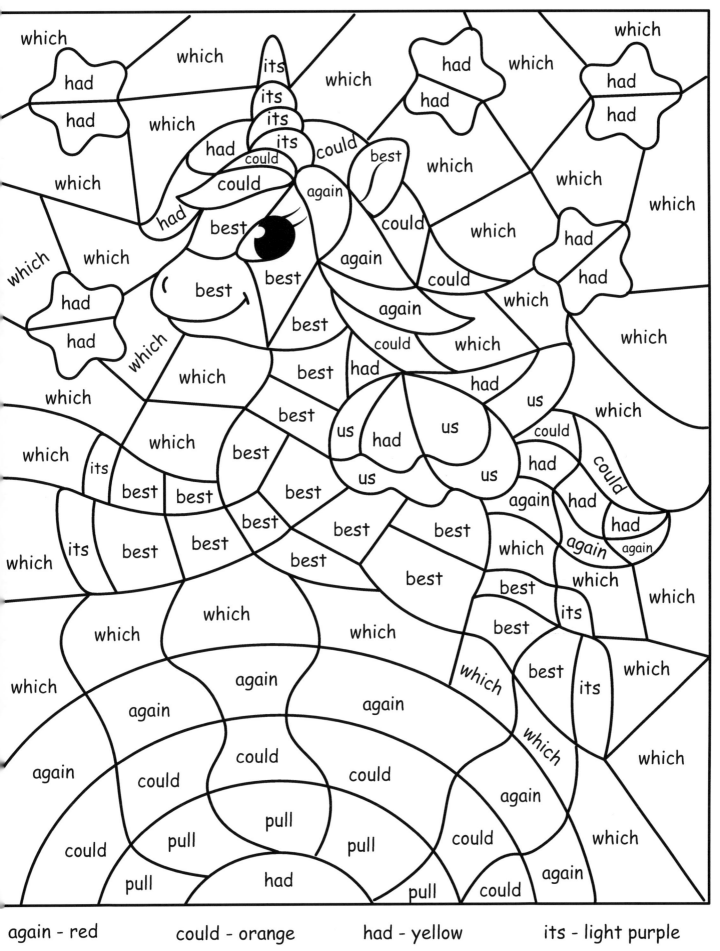

again - red    could - orange    had - yellow    its - light purple

best - light pink    us - dark pink    pull - light green    which - dark blue

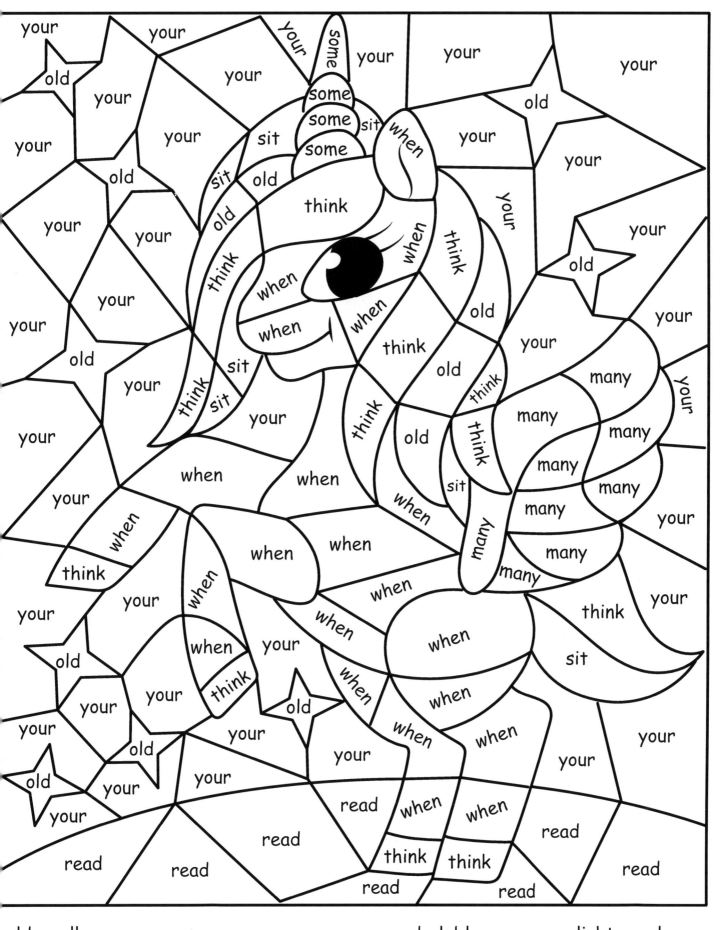

old - yellow     some - orange     your - dark blue     many - light purple

when - light pink     think - light blue     sit - dark purple     read - light green

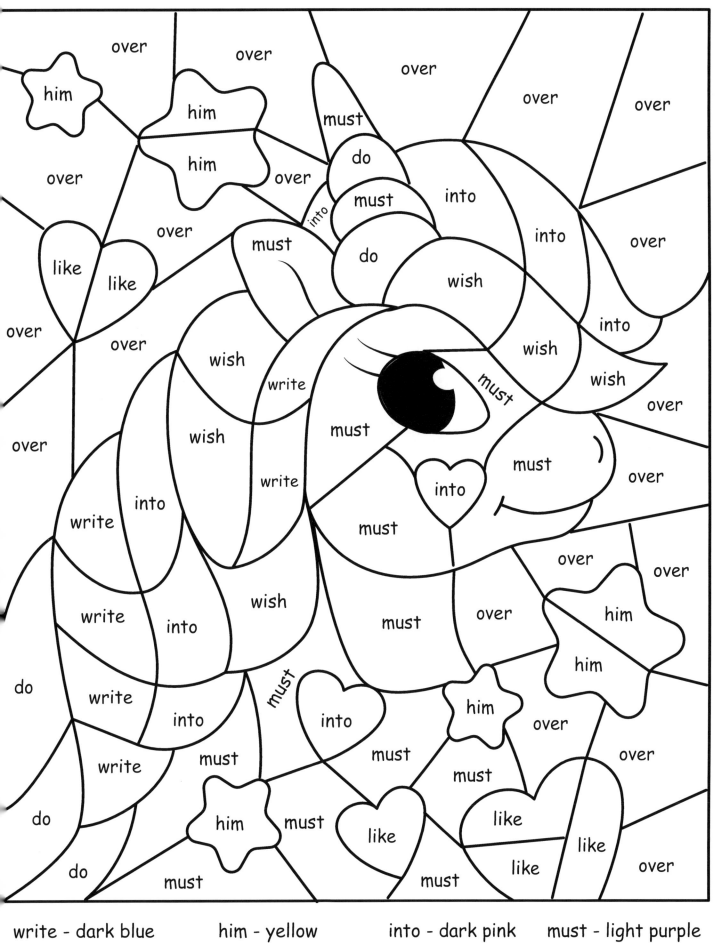

write - dark blue     him - yellow     into - dark pink     must - light purple

do - dark purple     over - light pink     like - red     wish - light blue

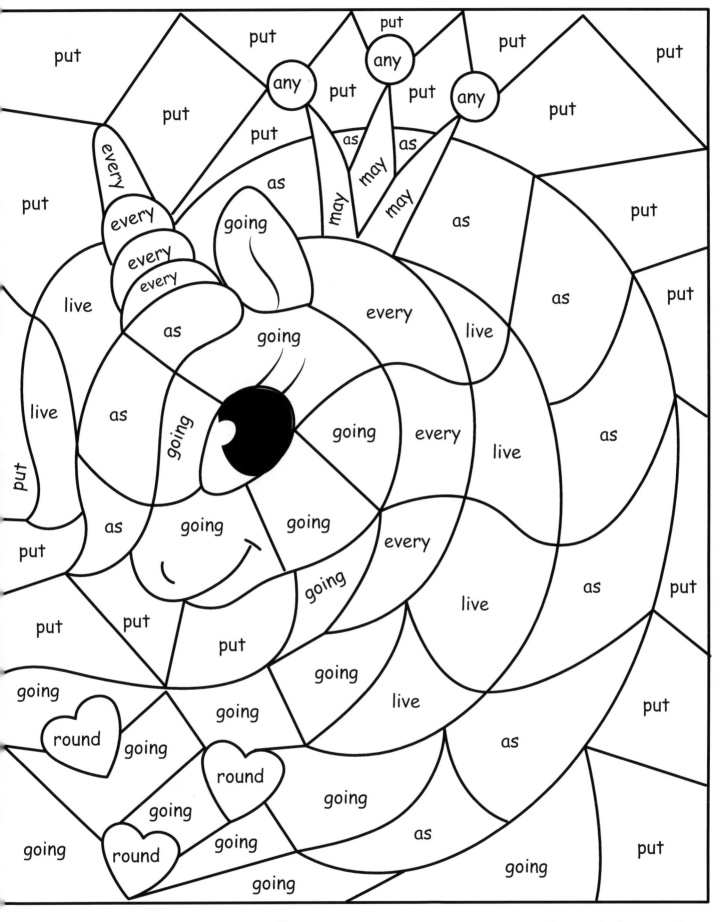

any - light green   going - yellow   may - orange   live - light purple

round - red   put - dark purple   every - dark pink   as - light pink

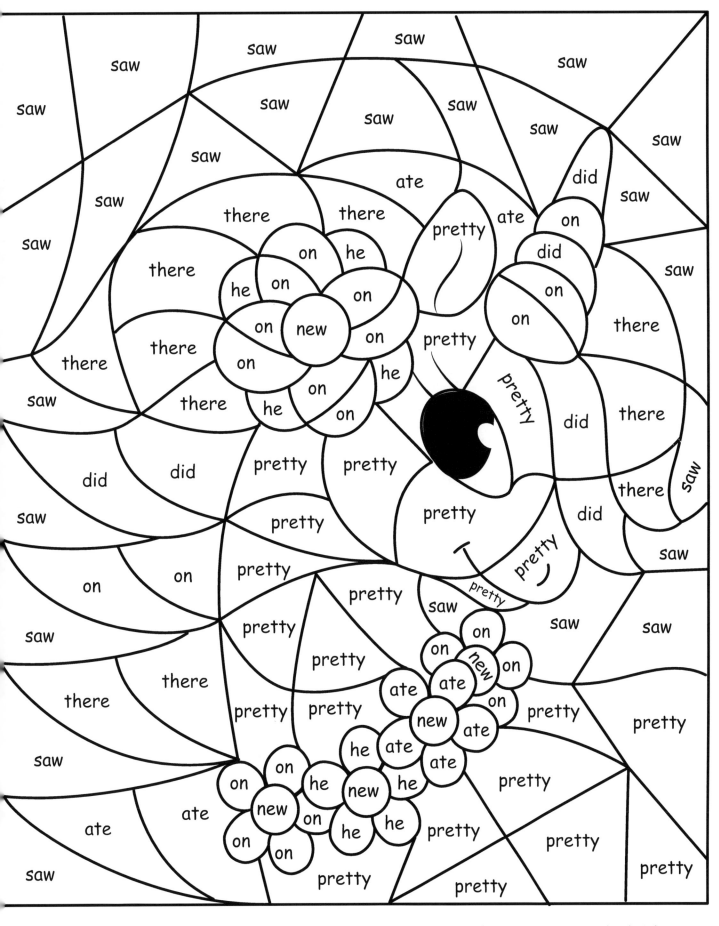

on - light pink    he - red    did - light purple    saw - dark blue

new - yellow    ate - dark purple    pretty - light blue    there - dark pink

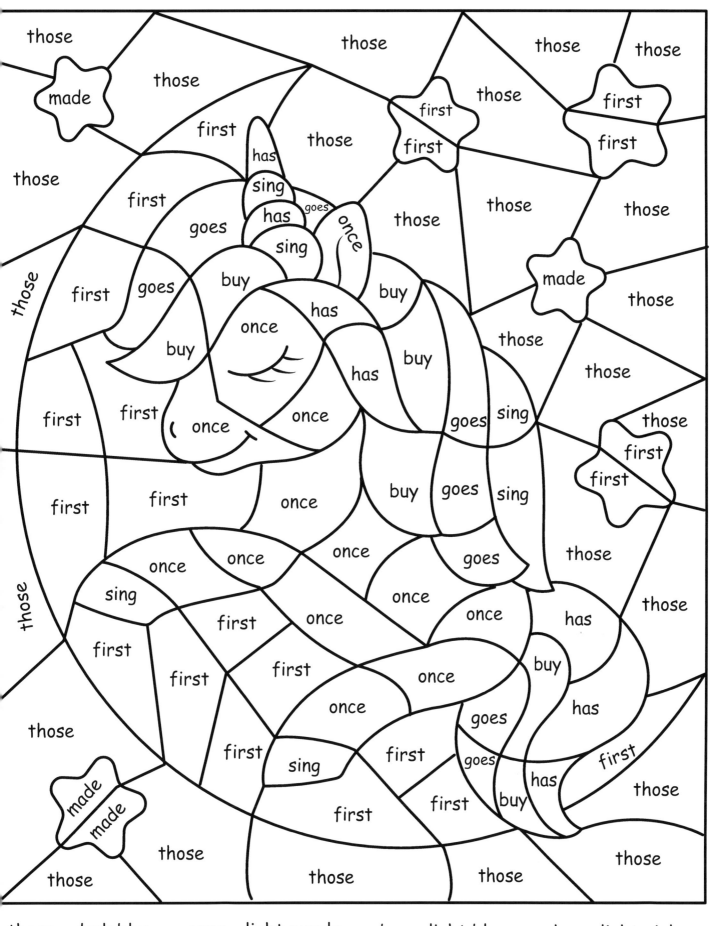

those - dark blue     once - light purple     buy - light blue     has - light pink

sing - dark purple     first - yellow     goes - dark pink     made - orange

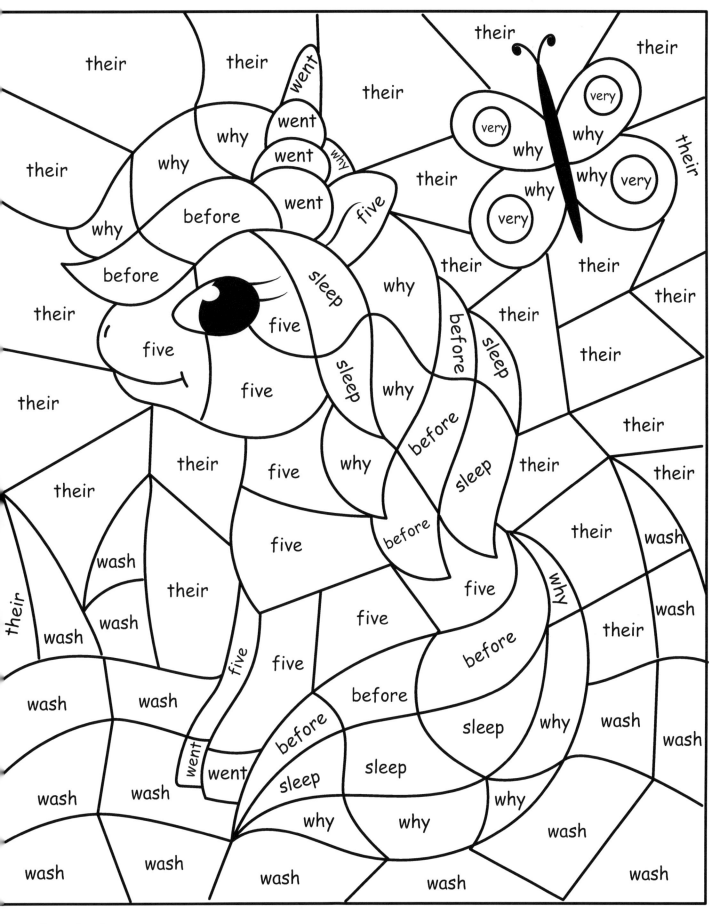

wash - dark green    five - yellow    before - red    why - orange
their - light blue    sleep - dark blue    very - light pink    went - light purple

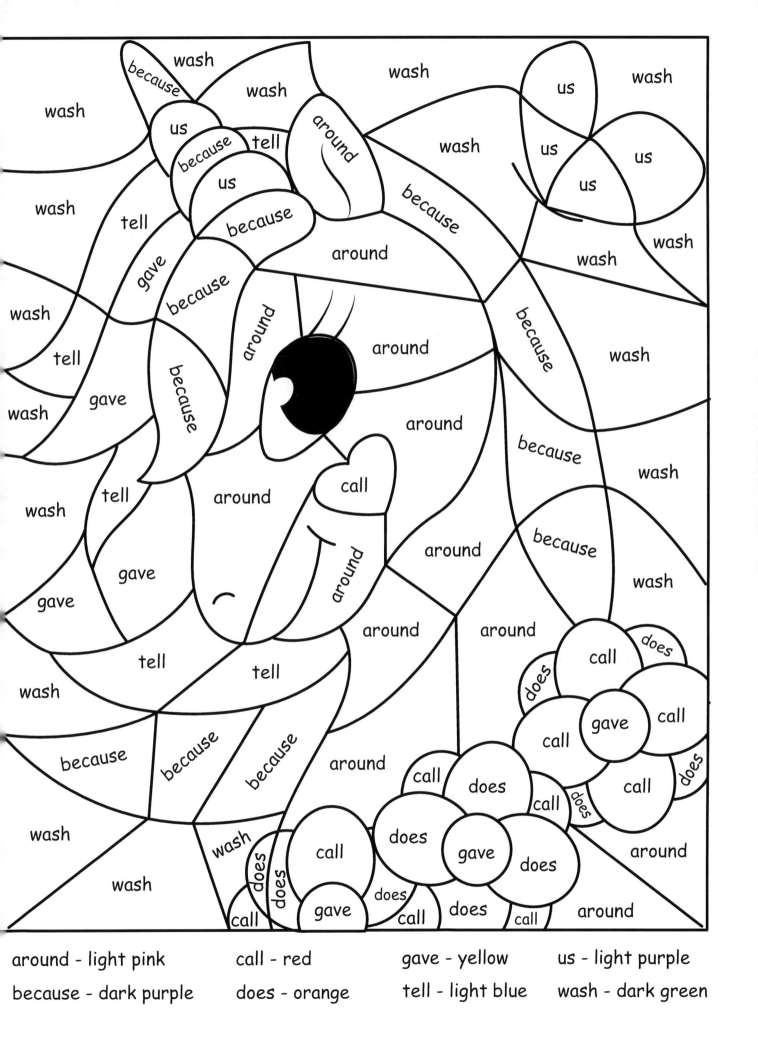

around - light pink    call - red    gave - yellow    us - light purple

because - dark purple    does - orange    tell - light blue    wash - dark green

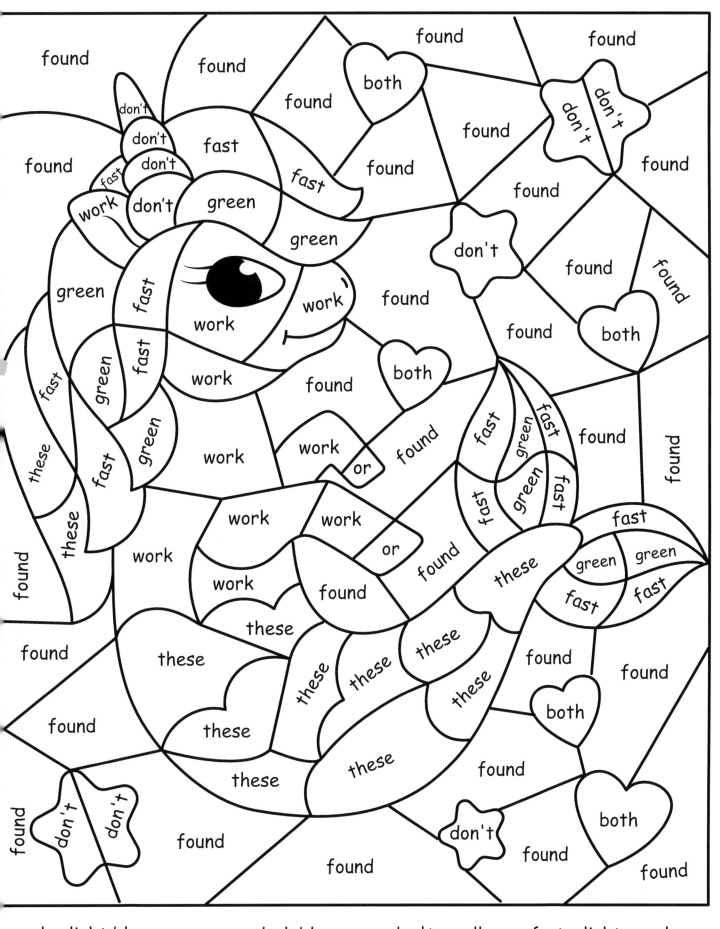

work - light blue    or - dark blue    don't - yellow    fast - light purple

these - dark purple    green - light pink    both - red    found - light green

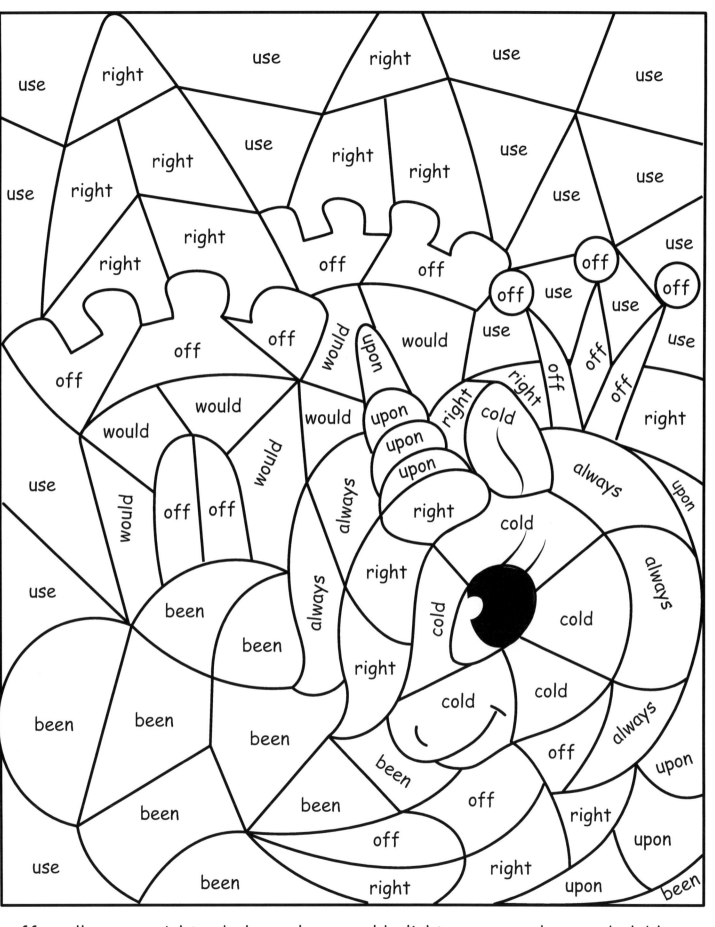

off - yellow     right - dark purple     would - light green     always - dark blue

cold - light pink     use - light blue     upon - dark pink     been - light purple

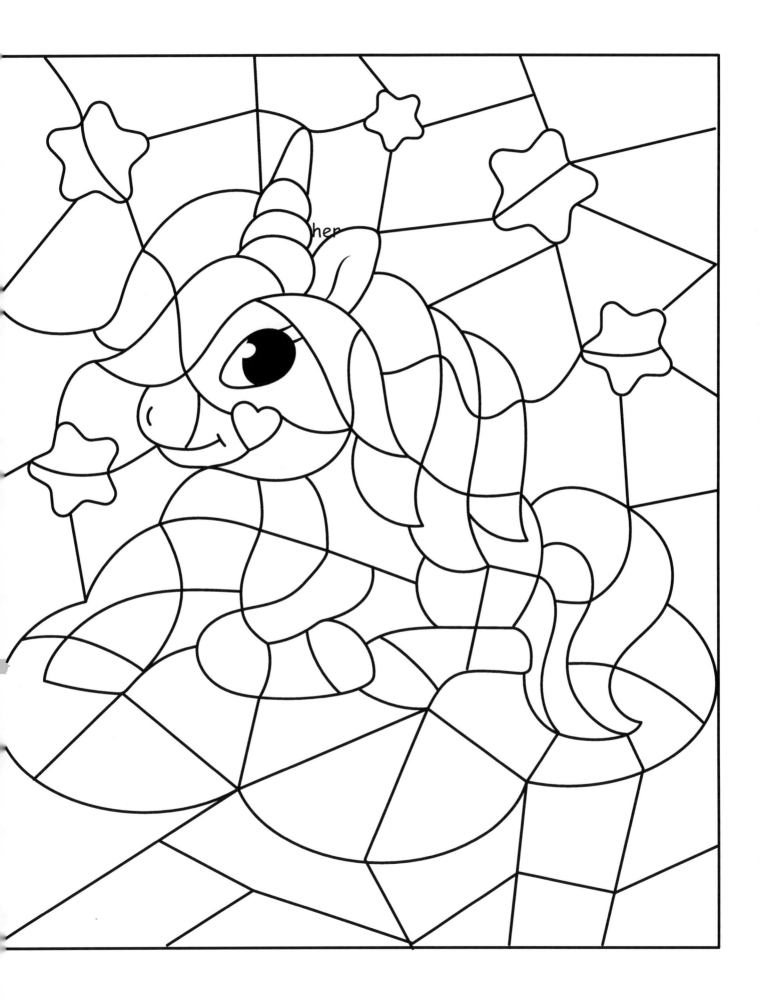

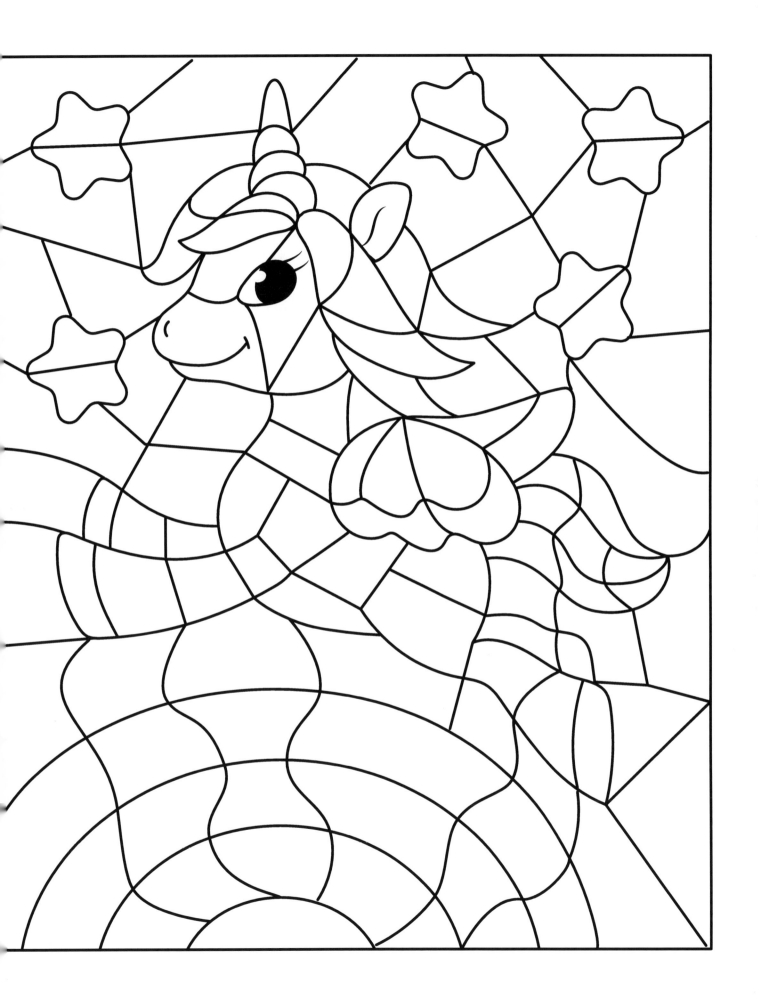

To download FREE color by number, color by sight word
and coloring pages, visit:
www.sparkling-minds.com

Made in the USA
Middletown, DE
09 July 2021